Hello!
I am a koala
and my name is Chomel.

I hope you will enjoy
looking at the pictures,
whilst reading and
learning all the words
in this book.

See you again!!

-Chomel-

Another great picture book
to share with children:

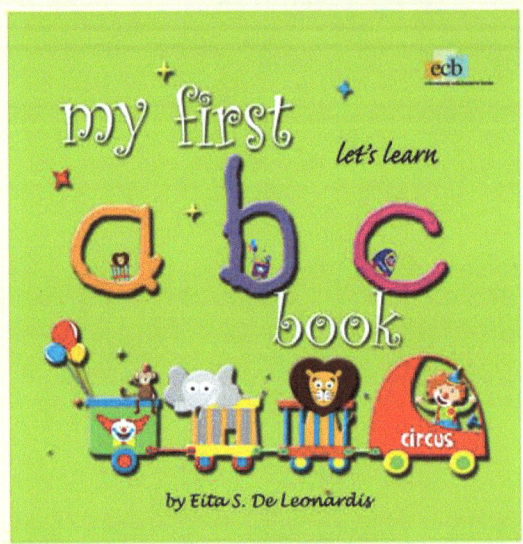

978-0-9568335-1-8

This book belongs to:
_____

Let's learn the words

by Eita S De Leonardis

first published in 2011
by ECB Publishing Ltd.

Text copyright©Eita S. De Leonardis
Illustration copyright©Eita S. De Leonardis

To Alia Zahra Daniyal De Leonardis,
my precious baby girl - MUMMY

ECB Publishing Ltd.
Connexion East, 1, 139 Marfleet Lane
Hull HU9 5RN
England

The right of Eita S. De Leonardis to be identified as the author and illustrator of this Work has been asserted by her in accordance with the Copyright, Designs and Patents Act 1998

All rights reserved

A catalogue record of this book is available from the British Library

ISBN 978-0-9568335-2-5

Credits to istock/o-che, istock/mubai, istock/russltadotcom istock/privatehand,

Printed in England

ECB Publishing Ltd. UK
www.ECB-Publishing.com

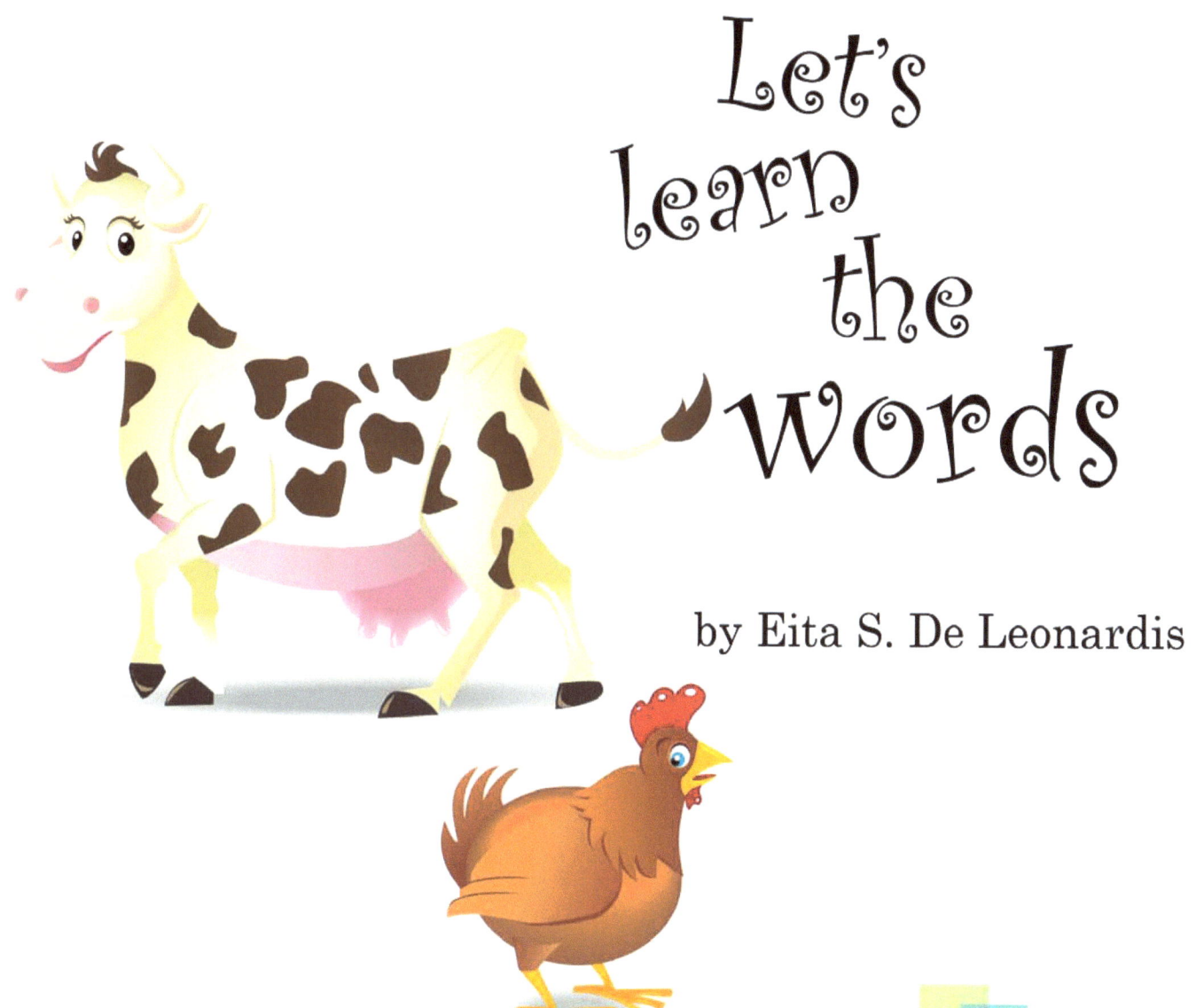

Let's learn the words

by Eita S. De Leonardis

ecb
educational collaborative books

crab	jellyfish	hats
cuttlefish	seahorse	coral
fish	starfish	turtle

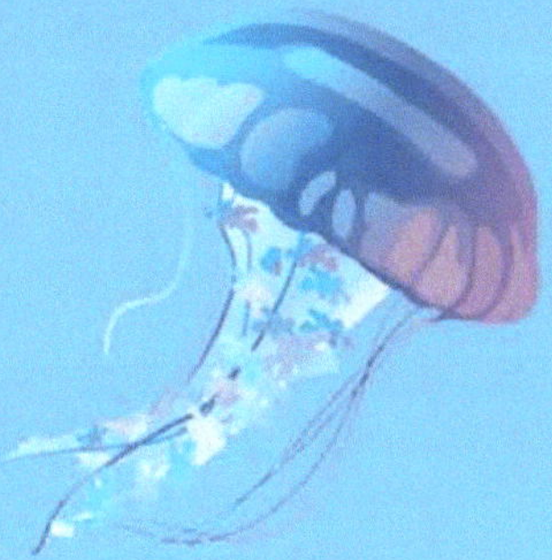

coffee maker grater cake mixer

pots oven glove rolling pin

kettle food blender spatulas

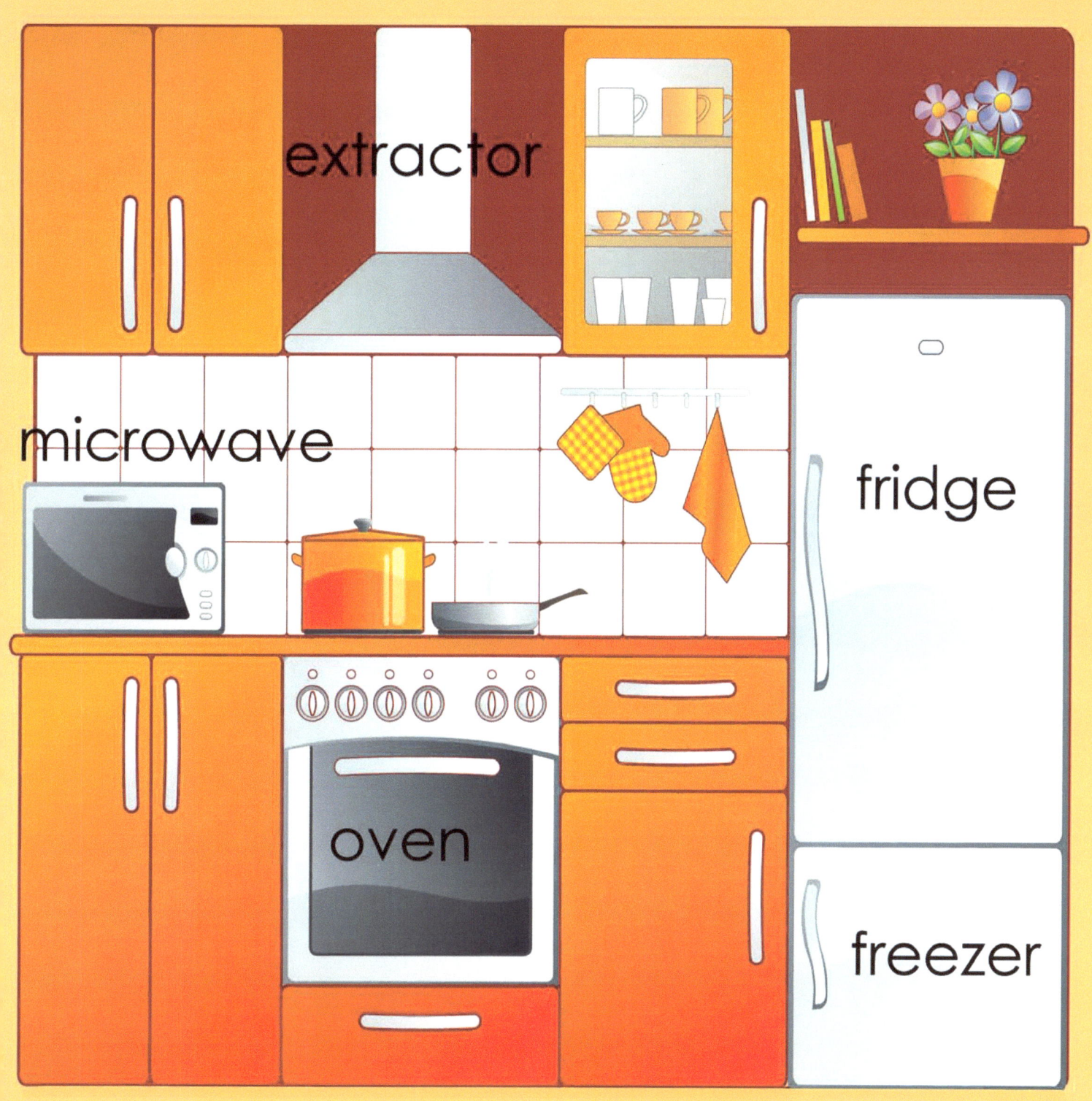

 pumpkin

 parsnip

 tomato

 cabbage

 potato

 bell pepper

 onion

 cauliflower

 garlic

camp fire

rucksack

lantern

map

wood logs

compass

canoe

water flask

camping tent

torchlight

binocular

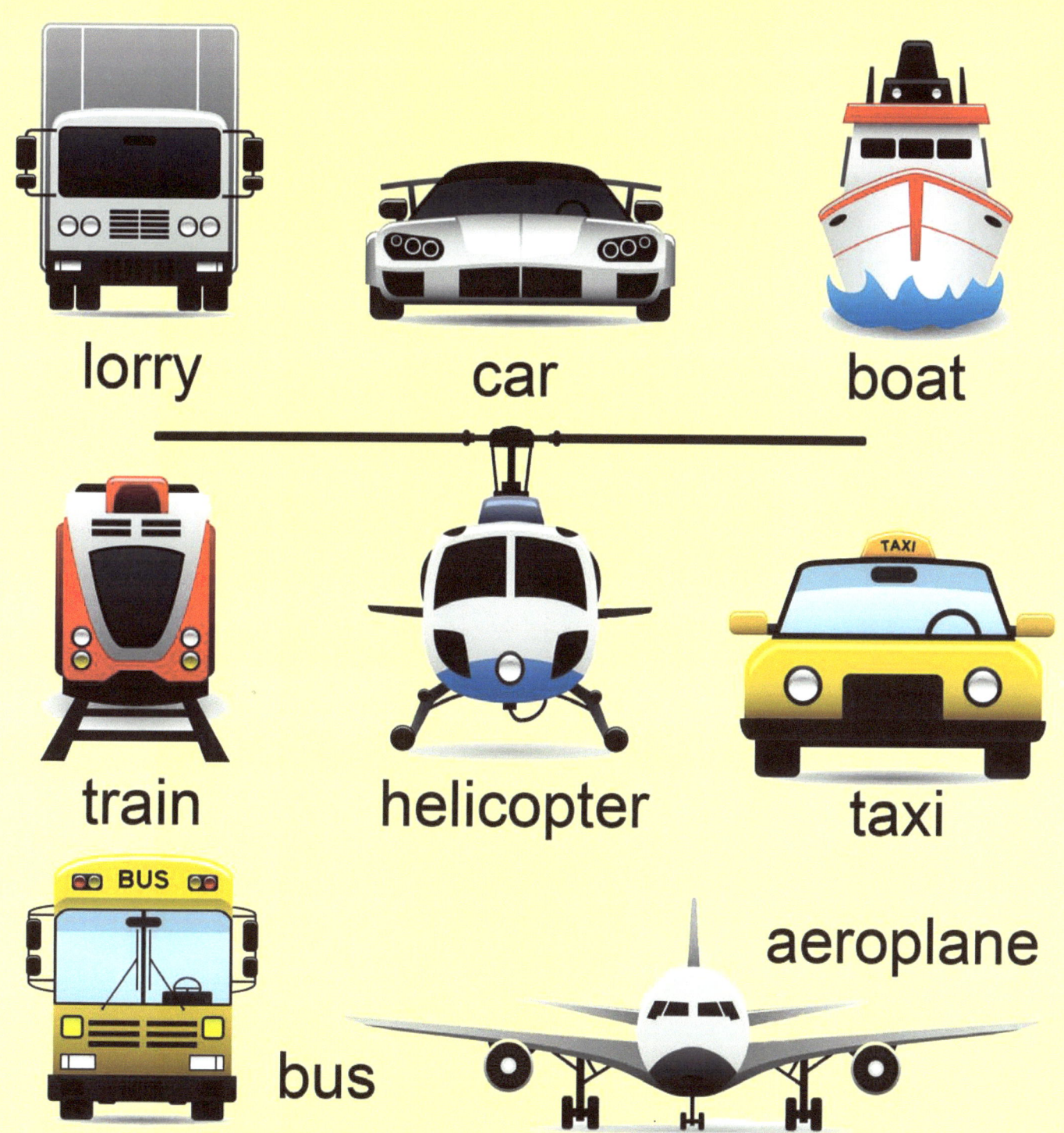

purple   red   green

black   yellow   blue

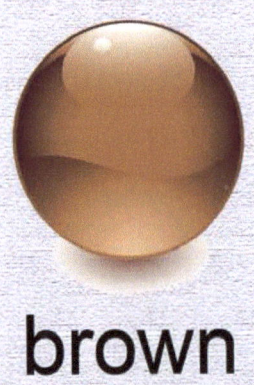  

brown   orange   white

flower shape

heart shape

circle

pentagon

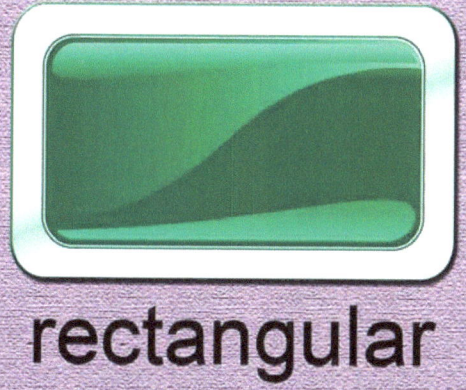
rectangular

star

Hi!
I guess you have
finished looking at all the
pictures whilst reading
and learning all the words
in this book.

I hope, you have enjoyed and
please, don't forget to come
back meeting me here
and reading this
book again soon.

Bye-bye and
see you again.

-Chomel-

www.ingramcontent.com/pod-product-compliance
Lightning Source LLC
Chambersburg PA
CBHW041233040426
42444CB00002B/147

About the Author

I am a high school student who enjoys playing squash, dancing, singing, and traveling. I live with my family and my dog in California. I love writing, drawing, and making videos especially for kids. My last few books were "Oops! I'm Early", "Yippee! I'm Home", and "Mask Up!"

More books in this series:

"Uh Oh! Gotta Go"

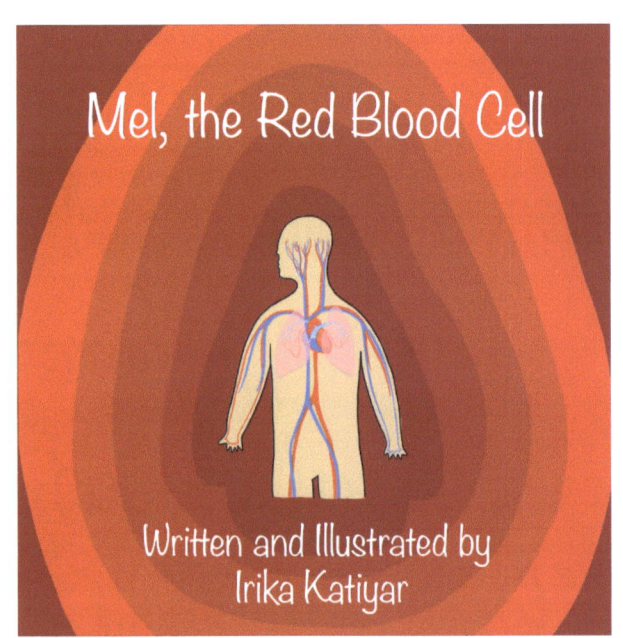

"Mel, the Red Blood Cell"

www.ingramcontent.com/pod-product-compliance
Lightning Source LLC
Chambersburg PA
CBHW041233040426
42444CB00002B/144